THIS BOOK BELONGS TO

Maeve Connick

St. Peter's Church, Glenburn

December 2023

LOOKING AHEAD

LOOKING

A Catholic Handbook for School Students

AHEAD

The Association of Catholic Women
in collaboration with the Catholic Truth Society

Nihil Obstat: The Reverend Monsignor Timothy Galligan
Imprimatur: The Reverend Monsignor Gerald Ewing VG
27th January 2023

The Nihil Obstat *and* Imprimatur *are a declaration that a publication is considered to be free from doctrinal or moral error. It is not implied that those who have granted the* Nihil Obstat *and* Imprimatur *agree with the contents, opinions or statements expressed.*

Looking Ahead edited by Joanna Bogle and Kyra Audley-Charles
All rights reserved.
First published 2023 by The Incorporated Catholic Truth Society
42-46 Harleyford Road London SE11 5AY
Tel: 020 7640 0042
Copyright © 2023 The Incorporated Catholic Truth Society
www.ctsbooks.org

ISBN 978 1 78469 747 1

Printed and bound by L.E.G.O. S.p.A., Italy.

Contents

Arise!

Testify joyfully that Christ is alive!
Spread his message of love and
salvation among your contemporaries,
at school and in the university, at work,
in the digital world, everywhere.

Pope Francis

Foreword

As the Lord Jesus leads us forward in hope, the Catholic Church continues to respond to his command to 'go and make disciples of all the nations.' (*Mt* 28:19) Learning what it means to be a disciple of Christ raises new questions about all kinds of things, not least for young people growing up in the Britain of the 21st century – questions about God and science, about men and women and why we are different, about the Church's role in history, as well as the age-old questions about the eternal truths which have been raised in each generation.

Looking Ahead addresses old and the new questions. It also brings together some of the greatest prayers from the Church's rich heritage, as well as offering crucial information on the great moral truths which are written into the human heart and set out clearly by God in the Ten Commandments.

This is a book to use as a point of reference, and for checking on information and ideas; but it's also a book simply for reading, for pondering its message, and as an aid for prayer. It has been specially designed as something to use regularly, and to keep as a lifelong gift.

Enjoy this book, treasure it, share it with friends – and keep it handy so that it becomes a real companion in the years ahead.

May God bless you, now and always

 ✠ John Wilson
Archbishop of Southwark

God has created me to do him some definite service; he has committed some work to me which he has not committed to another. I have my mission; I may never know it in this life, but I shall be told it in the next. I am a link in a chain, a bond of connection between persons. He has not created me for nought.

St John Henry Newman

Faith and History

Who is Jesus Christ?

Jesus Christ is the Son of God. The Sacred writings of the Bible tell us about him and everything about his life fulfilled all the promises made by God through the prophets to the Jewish people in the centuries before his birth. At every moment of every day the sacrament of the Eucharist that he instituted is taking place somewhere in the world, just as he commanded.

He lived in the Roman Empire where careful records were kept. We know when he was born because of the tax census that was taken at the time, and when he died, because his trial was before a particular Roman governor, the date of whose reign we know from records.

Part of being a Christian is finding out about him: his miracles, his death, his Resurrection, and the Church he founded. His name is known around the world – in fact, we calculate our calendar from his birth, so that the first century began on 1st January AD 1, with 'AD' standing for anno domini, 'the year of our Lord'.

How do we know Jesus Christ existed?

We know that Jesus Christ was born over 2,020 years ago, and yet we have more evidence about Christ than about most figures of that era. The pagan historian Tacitus, when describing Christianity, noted that "the founder of this sect, Christus, was put to death by the Roman procurator Pontius Pilate, during the reign of Tiberius".

And in AD 112, Pliny the Younger, Roman governor of Bithynia, described Christians gathering at dawn to sing hymns to Christ. It is clear that both Tacitus and Pliny knew that Jesus was an historical figure (like Queen Victoria or Winston Churchill), not a myth.

What is the Bible?

The Bible is the Word of God. God's revelation to his people of his existence, nature and will was recorded and preserved in a collection of books that was gathered together by the Church, and through which we learn the story of God's creation of the world, humanity's fall from grace, and God's loving plan for our salvation.

The Holy Spirit inspired the human authors of the 45 books in the 'Old Testament' and the 27 books in the 'New Testament'. These books contain history, poetry, allegories, wisdom and advice, and even letters (or 'epistles'). Together, they are known as the 'Sacred Scriptures', or simply 'the Bible'.

The term 'Gospel' comes from the New Testament word 'evangelion', which can be understood as 'good announcement': the 'Good News' of God sending his Son to bring us his saving grace.

Can we trust the Gospels?

Around the year AD 170, St Irenaeus, Bishop of Lyons, looked at this question. He was a disciple of Polycarp, Bishop of Smyrna, who was a disciple of St John the Evangelist. St Irenaeus explained that the four Gospels (named after their authors Matthew, Mark, Luke and John) were based on eye-witness testimony – from the stories of people who knew Jesus and his Apostles:

Matthew wrote the Gospel among the Hebrews, in their own language, while Peter and Paul were preaching the Gospel in Rome and founding the Church there. After their departure Mark, the disciple and interpreter of Peter, composed a written version of what Peter had preached. Then Luke, Paul's companion and disciple, committed his preaching to book form. Then John too, the disciple of the Lord, who had leaned upon his breast, published his Gospel while he was living at Ephesus in Asia.

The stupendous Good News...
the empty tomb...Jesus Christ is risen!

...And if Christ has not been raised, then our preaching is in vain and your faith is in vain. (1 Co 15:14)

Jesus's birth, death and Resurrection AD 1-c. AD 33

Apostles' mission to the known world

Persecutions of Christians 64-313

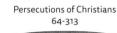

St Irenaeus of Ly c.130-c.202

50   100   150   200

Lindisfarne raided by Viking pirates 793

St Bede writes the history of the Church c.735

St Aidan found Lindisfarne 63

800   750   700   650

Pagan Viking invasions in Europe c.800-1066

St Elphege, Archbishop of Canterbury, martyred by Vikings 954-1011

Universities foun Bologna 1088 Oxford 1096, Pari

850   900   950   1000

Jesuit missions to the New World 1609-1763

Council of Trent 1545-1563

Henry VIII breaks with Rome 1534

Luther breaks with Rome 1517

Gutenber printing pres

1600   1550   1500   1450

St Peter's Basilica completed 1626

St Oliver Plunkett, martyred 1681

Catholic Relief Acts in Britain 1780s

St John Henry 1801-18

1650   1700   1750   1800

From Jesus to us...an unbroken line

...antine, first Christian ...peror c.272-c.337

St Alban, first British martyr, dies c.305

St Jerome 347-386

St Augustine of Hippo 354-430

250   300   350   400

St Augustine of ...terbury, died 604

Conversion of the Barbarians c.400-1000

Collapse of the Roman Empire 476

St Brigid of Kildare c.451-525

600   550   500   450

...eat East-West ...ism 1054

St Margaret of Scotland 1045-1093

The Crusades 1095-1291

St Thomas Becket, martyred 1170

St Richard of Chichester 1197-1253

1050   1100   1150   1200

Joan of Arc ...412-1431

St Julian of Norwich 1343-c.1416

Franciscan missions to China 1294-1368

St Thomas Aquinas 1225-1274

1400   1350   1300   1250

...tholic ...cipation ...ifts all ...ictions ...tain and ...nd 1829

1st Vatican Council 1869-1870

Apparitions of Our Lady: Lourdes 1858, Fatima 1917

2nd Vatican Council 1962-1965

St John Paul II 1920-2005

Bl Carlo Acutis 1991-2006

1850   1900   1950   2000

When did Christianity arrive in Britain?

Two thousand years ago, Britain was part of the Roman Empire – that same Roman Empire into which Christ was born. The Empire stretched across nearly all of what we today call Europe, as well as Asia Minor, much of North Africa and the Holy Land.

After Christ told his Apostles to go out and spread the Good News to all nations, they set out to do just that, and they gathered other missionaries to help them.

We don't know the names of the first Christians to arrive in Britain, but it was certainly in Roman times. A legend says that it was a small group led by Joseph of Arimithea, the man who provided the tomb for Christ's body to be laid in. The group is said to have landed on the

ROMAN EMPIRE c.117 AD

CANTERBURY

western coast of Britain, at Glastonbury in Somerset – then a marshy district where boats drew in from the sea – but so far there is no reliable evidence for that story.

It is certainly a fact that there was trade between western Britain and the rest of the Roman Empire. For example, tin from Cornwall was sold as far away as the Middle East.

Christianity flourished here in Britain as it did in the rest of the Roman Empire. When the Empire collapsed, pagan Angles and Saxons invaded from across the North Sea, taking over what came to be known as England. Christianity survived in western areas, including what we today call Wales and Cornwall. In their turn, the Saxons were converted to Christianity by missionaries sent from Rome, including St Augustine of Canterbury. When he arrived in Britain in the seventh century, Augustine encountered strong groups of Christians whose history dated back to Roman times.

Britain's patron saints

St Andrew was an Apostle, the brother of St Peter. There is no evidence that he actually preached in Scotland, although he certainly travelled long distances as, along with the other Apostles, he worked to spread the message of the Gospels. He died as a martyr around AD 60, crucified on an X-shaped cross. This is why the X-shape used on the Scottish flag is known as the Cross of St Andrew.

St Andrew's relics were brought to Scotland sometime in the fourth century; and Scots have had a strong devotion to him ever since.

Jesus calls his first disciples

While walking by the Sea of Galilee, he saw two brothers, Simon (who is called Peter) and Andrew his brother, casting a net into the sea, for they were fishermen. And he said to them, "Follow me, and I will make you fishers of men." Immediately they left their nets and followed him. (Mt 4:18-20)

The Lord's Prayer in Gaelic

Ar n-Athair a tha air nèamh,
Gu naomhaichear d'ainm.
Thigeadh do rìoghachd.
Dèanar do thoil air an talamh,
mar a nìthear air nèamh.
Tabhair dhuinn an-diugh
    ar n-aran làitheil.
Agus maith dhuinn ar fiachan,
amhail a mhaitheas sinne dar luchd-fiach.
Agus na leig ann am buaireadh sinn;
ach saor sinn o olc. Amen.

St Patrick was born in the first half of the fifth century, in Roman Britain – probably in what we today call Wales, at that time the very edge of the collapsing Roman Empire. His family had been Christian for several generations at least. Captured at the age of 16 by brigands from pagan Ireland and enslaved there, Patrick eventually made his escape, but was determined to return to convert the inhabitants of the island to Christianity. This he did after studying to become a priest, establishing the Church firmly in Ireland by converting thousands of pagans through his missionary work.

The Lord's Prayer in Irish

Ár n-Athair atá ar neamh,
Go naofar d'ainim,
Go dtagfadh do ríocht,
Go ndéantar do thoil ar an talamh
mar a dhéantar ar neamh.
Ár n-arán laethúil tabhair dúinn inn
agus maith dúinn ár bhfiacha
mar a mhaithimidne dár bhféichiúna féin
Ach ná lig sinn i gcathú,
ach saor sinn ó olc. Amen.

Did you know?

St Patrick used the shamrock, with its three leaves, to explain the doctrine of the Holy Trinity: Father, Son and Holy Spirit are three persons, but one God. To this day the shamrock is the symbol of Ireland.

St David lived in the sixth century in Wales and seems to have been a grandson of the king Ceredig ap Cunedda, king of Ceredigion. He preached and established monasteries in Wales and across the sea in Brittany, France, and is said to have founded the famous abbey at Glastonbury.

His monasteries were strict: the monks ate only bread and herbs and drank water, and pulled their own ploughs without oxen. The city of St David's was established where he was buried.

St David's blessing

St David's final words were a blessing to his community:

Be joyful, keep your faith and your creed, and do the little things that you have seen and heard me do.

Byddwch lawen, cadwch y ffydd a gwnewch y pethau bychain a welsoch ac a glywsoch gennyf i.

The Lord's Prayer in Welsh

Ein Tad yn y nefoedd,
sancteiddier dy enw;
deled dy deyrnas;
gwneler dy ewyllys,
ar y ddaear fel yn y nef.
Dyro inni heddiw ein bara beunyddiol,
a maddau inni ein troseddau,
fel yr ŷm ni wedi maddau i'r rhai a
    droseddodd yn ein herbyn;
a phaid â'n dwyn i brawf,
ond gwared ni rhag yr Un drwg. Amen.

St George was a Roman soldier, martyred under the pagan Emperor Diocletian in the fourth century in the Middle East. English soldiers learned his story when they travelled to the Holy Land during the Crusades of the eleventh century.

The soldiers adopted St George as a patron and made him a popular saint, although there were also churches dedicated to him in Britain before that time.

The Lord's Prayer in English

Our Father, who art in heaven,
hallowed be thy name.
Thy Kingdom come.
Thy will be done on earth
as it is in heaven.
Give us this day our daily bread,
and forgive us our trespasses,
as we forgive those who trespass against us,
and lead us not into temptation,
but deliver us from evil. Amen.

Did you know?

The flag of the United Kingdom, the Union Jack, is formed of three heraldic crosses: the cross saltire of St Andrew, patron saint of Scotland, the cross of St George, patron saint of England, and the cross saltire of St Patrick, patron saint of Ireland.

The Reformation in Britain

The Church in medieval Britain was strong and powerful. Everyone was baptised and was expected to live as a Catholic and practise their Catholic faith. There were magnificent cathedrals and parish churches. Monasteries and convents across the country cared for the poor and sick. But the Church could also be stern, and the power and privileges of the bishops and other important people could also bring corruption and laziness.

The Church needed reforming. By the start of the 1500s there was a sense of times changing and new challenges. But some of those who sought reform went too far and got mixed up in political and doctrinal arguments. This led to attempts to change important beliefs that Christians had held from the earliest days, for example the central truths about the Eucharist and about Mary, the Mother of God.

Some key dates:

1534: King Henry VIII broke with the Pope and announced that he was the head of the Church in England.

In England, the issues were dominated by politics. King Henry VIII, seeking to divorce his wife as he believed a new wife would bring him the son he badly wanted, announced himself as head of the Church and broke with the Pope. He closed all the monasteries and took their lands.

After the death of Henry VIII and during the reigns of Edward VI, Mary I and Elizabeth I, things see-sawed between Catholicism and Protestantism, as each monarch sought to impose religious unity. Under Queen Mary, Protestants were burned alive; under Elizabeth I, Catholics were tortured, hanged and dismembered.

Over the following centuries, Catholics continued to be persecuted: practising the Catholic faith was illegal, and those who refused to renounce their beliefs – the 'recusants' – could be executed. Priests were ordained in exile and returned to Britain in secret to minister to faithful Catholics. There were heroic priests such as Saints John Fisher and John Southworth, as well as many devoted lay people such as Saints Thomas More, Margaret Clitherow, Anne Line and Nicholas Owen, who died as martyrs.

1535: Sir Thomas More, chancellor of England, and Bishop John Fisher, Bishop of Rochester, refused to affirm the King's claim to be head of the Church. Both were martyred on 22nd June 1535 at Tower Hill in London. Today they are both honoured as saints.

"I die the king's good servant – but God's first."
St Thomas More's last words

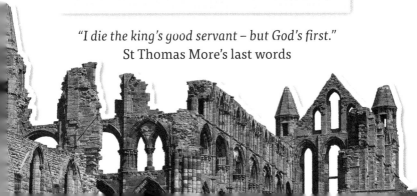

Catholics were only given equal rights in 1829, and today the state no longer dictates which faith people must believe, so we are free once more to live and worship as Catholics, according to the truth.

Did you know?

During the persecution of Catholics, it was an act of High Treason for a priest to even enter the country! Still, brave priests were determined to minister to those in England who secretly remained Catholic. A carpenter and lay Jesuit brother named Nicholas Owen worked on a network of safe houses where priests could stay in secret. He was brilliant at building hiding places known as 'priest holes' into these houses, so that when the 'priest hunters' came around, the priests could shelter, undetected, behind a hidden door or in a secret passage. Nicholas Owen's priest holes were so cleverly constructed that Fr Henry Garnet was able to live and minister in Baddesley Clinton House in Warwickshire (shown below) for fourteen years without being discovered by the priest hunters!

Good news across the world

Elsewhere in the world, the history of the Catholic Church followed a very different course – one of startling growth. In 1531, just as the Reformation was tearing the Christians of Europe apart, Our Lady appeared to an indigenous Mexican man called Juan Diego. A miraculous image of Our Lady appeared on his cloak, which can still be seen in the Basilica of Our Lady of Guadalupe in northern Mexico. Our Lady's apparition gave a new impetus to missionary activity in Central and South America, and in the next ten years over ten million people converted to Christianity.

In Asia, Catholic explorers such as Magellan from Portugal (the first person to circumnavigate the globe) sailed with missionary priests who undertook the conversion of some of the countries of the world that now have the most Catholics, for example the Philippines. Great Jesuit missionaries such as St Francis Xavier went out to preach the Gospel in South India, Japan and as far as China. St Francis is said to have baptised more than 700,000 people with his own hands. His body is still revered in a Church in Goa; however, in terms of numbers, his missionary efforts in Japan and China did not meet with the same success.

Today, the fastest growing region for the Catholic Church is Africa, especially the countries of West Africa, such as Nigeria, Ghana and Zambia. There are over 200 million Catholics in Africa, which is equivalent to one in five Catholics in the world. During the nineteenth century, missionaries from France and Ireland travelled to Africa, preaching the message of the Gospels and opening schools and hospitals across the continent. Today, more than a quarter of men training to be priests come from African countries.

Following the suppression of the Faith during the Reformation, the Catholic Church in Britain began to revive in the late eighteenth and nineteenth centuries. One leading figure of that time was St John Henry Newman, a Church of England clergyman who became a Catholic. A number of remarkable women, including Frances Taylor, Elizabeth Prout and Cornelia Connolly, established new religious orders in Britain. The Church's work in education and with the poor expanded rapidly: by the middle of the twentieth century there was a network of parishes and Catholic schools across the country.

In 1982, Pope John Paul II was the first pope ever to visit Britain. He met Queen Elizabeth II, prayed with Anglicans at Canterbury and addressed large crowds at London, Coventry, Edinburgh, Liverpool and Cardiff among other places.

In 2010, Pope Benedict XVI made a state visit at the invitation of Queen Elizabeth II. He beatified John Henry Newman at an open-air Mass and addressed civic and political figures gathered in the Houses of Parliament.

God is not a scientific explanation.
If you are using God instead of science
to explain what happens in the
[natural] world you are talking about
the gods of the Romans and Greeks.
We believe in a God that creates
outside of space and time and shows
us everything he did. We experience
God as a person, as a god of love.

Brother Guy Consolmagno, SJ
Director of the Vatican Observatory

Our World
and Science

Genesis: the beginning...his love

God brought everything into existence, including the earth and all the stars and planets – the whole immense universe. In the Book of Genesis, the first book of the Bible, his creation of everything is all described lyrically, emphasising a sense of order and meaning and purpose. God made humanity – man and woman – as the peak of creation, "in his own image". His plan was to have a special, close relationship with humans.

God is the author of time itself. We may wonder about how long it all took – the era of dinosaurs, the slow evolution of various creatures – but what the Sacred Scriptures teach us is that it was all ordered and had a purpose: his plan was to bring human beings into existence to share his love. He created them to know and serve him and to be happy for ever.

But... You must have noticed that some things are not right in our world, and that nobody's perfect.

Why is this? The Book of Genesis also shows us that God made man and woman free: free to choose whether or not to respond to his love. They chose to disobey, and this brought misery and confusion into everything. Despite this 'Original Sin' of man and woman, God's plan did not change: he still wanted to have a close, loving relationship. However, humanity's relationship with God required restoration. In order to achieve this, God promised to send a saviour – his only Son – to be born to the Blessed Virgin Mary and to live among us, as one of us, as the man Jesus Christ, to bear upon his own shoulders the burdens and sufferings of sinners, and to restore our union with God.

This responsibility for God's earth means
that human beings, endowed with
intelligence, must respect the laws of nature
and the delicate equilibria existing
between the creatures of this world,
for "he commanded and they were created;
and he established them for ever and ever;
he fixed their bounds and he set a law
which cannot pass away" (Ps 148:5b-6).

Pope Francis
Laudato Si' 68

Our world

God cares about each one of us much more than we can ever imagine. Much more than our mum or our dad, or our family, or our best friend. And he is very near, so close that he knows all that we feel and do and think.

That first disobedience of man and woman, the Original Sin, is sometimes called the 'Fall'. In order to lift us up again, God came to join in his creation. He came to live among us: Jesus Christ, the Saviour of the world. Through him, and his death and Resurrection, we are healed and sins are forgiven. But that original Fall wounded our world and each one of us. We can see this all around us: in small things such as unkindness or spitefulness, and in larger ones such as war or the destruction of our environment. We need to co-operate with God, and with one another, to help things to work well for the good of all – and we have been given the ability to do this, to solve difficulties, and even achieve great things. We do not need to be afraid: God's love is huge, and we have been given great gifts.

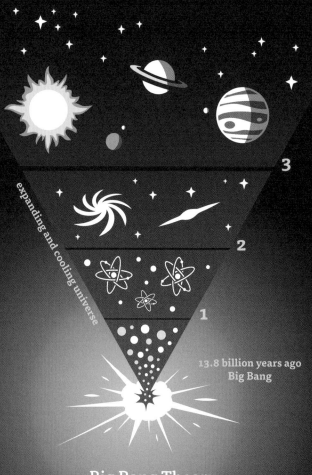

expanding and cooling universe

4

3

2

1

13.8 billion years ago
Big Bang

Big Bang Theory

1	2	3	4
First seconds after Big Bang birth of subatomic particles	380,000 years later electrons and nuclei combined into atoms	300 million years later beginning formation of the stars and galaxies	9 billion years later beginning formation of the solar system and earth

What is the big bang theory?

A Catholic priest first hypothesised the 'big bang'. This is the theory that the observable universe began with the explosion of a single dense particle at one moment in time. Georges Lemaître (1894-1966), born in Belgium, was ordained in 1923 after serving as a soldier in World War I. He studied mathematics and astronomy in Europe and America, gaining his PhD from the Massachusetts Institute of Technology.

When he published his big-bang theory in 1931 it challenged much of the traditional thinking, by explaining that the universe was in fact expanding and not static. But it was the result of years of research, and it followed the work of other scientists, including Albert Einstein and Edwin Hubble. Today, most astronomers accept the theory: Lemaître had opened the way for a new approach. He was awarded a number of international prizes for science, and he was also a noted linguist and musician.

Find out more here:

www.physicsoftheuniverse.com/scientists_lemaitre.html

The Church and evolution

Some people assume that the Catholic Church completely rejects the theory of evolution because of the accounts of creation in Genesis. However, this isn't actually true. In 1950, when Charles Darwin's theory of evolution was less than 100 years old, Pope Pius XII declared that there was no opposition between the theory of evolution and Catholic teaching, provided both were properly understood.

Recently Pope Francis adopted a similar position, saying: "The evolution in nature is not opposed to the notion of creation, because evolution presupposes the creation of beings that evolve." In other words, evolution doesn't rule out creation by God. (After all, even if life on earth evolved over millions of years, all the 'stuff' that evolved had to come from *somewhere*!)

Pope St John Paul II pointed out that we know that God created humanity in his own image, so any theory about where people come from has to involve more than just a material process. And Pope Benedict XVI said that the theory of evolution was in fact very useful in understanding reality, provided we kept in mind that it can't answer *all* our questions about human origins:

> [The debate between creationism and evolutionism] is absurd because, on the one hand, there are so many scientific proofs in favour of evolution which appears to be a reality we can see and which enriches our knowledge of life and being as such. But on the other, the doctrine of evolution does not answer every query, especially the great philosophical question: where does everything come from? And how did everything start which ultimately led to man?

The wasting of creation begins when
we no longer recognise any need superior
to our own, but see only ourselves.
It begins when there is no longer any concept
of life beyond death, where in this life we must
grab hold of everything and possess life as
intensely as possible, where we must possess
all that is possible to possess.

Pope Benedict XVI
Address to the Clergy of the Diocese of
Bolzano-Bressanone, 6th August 2008

Noted Catholic Scientists

Many people think that faith and science do not mix; however, the work of Catholic scientists throughout the ages tells a different story. Here are some examples of Catholics who have made great contributions to science.

Hildegard of Bingen (c.1098-c.1179)
A nun who pioneered an understanding of a proper balance in life, caring for mental, emotional, physical and spiritual health. She was also a noted herbalist discovering cures that, in various forms, we still use today.

Roger Bacon (c.1214-c.1294)
A Franciscan friar who has been described as the forerunner of the modern scientific method, doing scientific research by using observation to develop hypotheses and then testing them by conducting different experiments.

Leonardo da Vinci (1452-1519)
A layman, he was an anatomist, scientist and inventor as well as a famous painter.

Nicholas Copernicus (1473-1543)
A priest whose discovery that the earth moves around the sun created the 'Copernican revolution'.

Albert Curtz (1600-1671)
A Jesuit priest and astronomer: the Curtius crater on the moon is named after him.

Athanasius Kircher (1602-1680)
A Jesuit priest who was one of the first people to observe microbes through a microscope and to recognise that diseases are caused by micro-organisms.

Jean Picard (1620-1682)
A priest who was the first person to measure the diameter of the sun with some accuracy. The Picard satellite, which orbited the earth performing solar observations between 2010 and 2014, was named after him.

Nicholas Steno (1638-1686)
A Danish priest who discovered that the heart is a muscle and was also the founder of the modern science of geology.

Georg Joseph Kamel (1661-1706)
A Jesuit missionary and botanist: the flower Camellia is named after him.

Maria Gaetana Agnesi (1718-1799)
The first female professor of mathematics in the world, she was appointed to the faculty of the University of Bologna by Pope Benedict XIV and wrote the first book discussing differential and integral calculus.

Louis Braille (1809-1852)
Blinded in a childhood accident, he created the Braille alphabet to allow the blind to read by touch using a pattern of raised dots.

Louis Pasteur (1822-1895)
A biologist who created vaccines for rabies and anthrax.

Alois Alzheimer (1864-1915)
A physician who identified the dementia that now bears his name.

Georges Lemaître (1894-1966)
A Belgian priest, astronomer and physicist who first proposed the big-bang theory.

Jérôme Lejeune (1926-1994)
A geneticist who discovered the cause of Down's syndrome.

And there are many, many more!
Check out Wikipedia's list of Catholic clergy scientists and its list of lay Catholic scientists too.

Dear young people,
listen to his voice. Do not be afraid.
Open up your hearts to Christ.
The deepest joy there is in life is the joy
that comes from God and is found
in Jesus Christ, the Son of God.
He is the hope of the world.
Jesus Christ is your hope and mine!

Pope St John Paul II

Young Saints

Pope Benedict XVI speaks to the young people of Britain

When he visited the UK in 2010, Pope Benedict chose as his theme the famous motto of St John Henry Newman: "Heart speaks unto heart". In his Message to Young People delivered in Westminster Cathedral, he spoke about what these words mean for today's youth:

> I ask each of you…to look into your own heart. Think of all the love that your heart was made to receive, and all the love it is meant to give. After all, we were made for love. This is what the Bible means when it says that we are made in the image and likeness of God: we were made to know the God of love, the God who is Father, Son and Holy Spirit, and to find our supreme fulfilment in that divine love that knows no beginning or end. We were made to receive love, and we have. Every day we should thank God for the love we have already known, for the love that has made us who we are, the love that has shown us what is truly important in life…

We were also made to give love, to make love the inspiration for all we do, and the most enduring thing in our lives. At times this seems so natural, especially when we feel the exhilaration of love, when our hearts brim over with generosity, idealism, the desire to help others, to build a better world. But at other times, we realise that it is difficult to love... Every day we have to choose to love, and this requires help...

This is the message I want to share with you today. I ask you to look into your hearts, each day, to find the source of all true love. Jesus is always there... Even amid the 'busy-ness' and the stress of our daily lives, we need to make space for silence, because it is in silence that we find God, and in silence that we discover our true self. And in discovering our true self, we discover the particular vocation which God has given us for the building up of his Church and the redemption of our world.

Heart speaks unto heart. With these
words from my heart, dear young friends,
I assure you of my prayers for you...

Pope Benedict XVI

Carlo Acutis

Carlo Acutis was a teenage computer and football enthusiast who opened up to millions of people an understanding of what Holy Communion really is. He was born in London in 1991, to an Italian family who weren't regular churchgoers.

As he grew up, he sought to know more about the Faith, leading to his discovery of the Eucharist, which, according to him, brings us close to Christ and is a "foretaste of heaven". He used his computer skills to teach people about the Eucharist – Christ truly present under the appearance of bread and wine – and some of the dramatic miracles associated with it.

An active and strong-minded boy, Carlo showed great courage when he learned that he had leukaemia – a form of cancer – and he refused to complain. Instead, he offered it all up "for the Pope and the Church and for people who are suffering".

He died aged only fifteen in 2006, and thousands of young people came from all over the world when he was laid in a special tomb in Assisi, Italy. They were inspired by his example and by the way he used the internet to show the truth about Holy Communion: "a highway to heaven". In 2020 he was declared "Blessed".

Carlo Acutis said "Sadness is the gaze directed inwards, while happiness is the gaze directed towards God."

Charles Lwanga and companions

Charles Lwanga and companions were teenagers, training as royal guards at the court of the Kabaka, the ruler of the kingdom of Buganda in Africa in the late-nineteenth century.

Missionaries from Britain and elsewhere had brought the great message of Christianity, and the teenagers were among the first to ask to be baptised. The Kabaka was interested too, but he feared that people might think he was being weak if he became a Christian, and he didn't like the fact that the Christian boys would not take part in homosexual acts with him.

One day he became particularly angry and called on all "those who pray" to stand forward. Charles Lwanga and twenty-four others did so. The Kabaka had them arrested and chained and forced to march for days without food or water to a traditional execution site at Namugongo, where they were burned alive. The youngest, Kizito, was just fourteen.

Today there are millions of Christians in Uganda. The feast day of the young martyrs (3rd June) is a holiday for all Ugandans. Africa is becoming the most Christian continent in the world.

We can ask the help of the Ugandan martyrs when we are attacked for our Christian beliefs.

Dominic Savio

Dominic Savio was born into a poor family in Italy in 1842. His father was a blacksmith, and his mother worked at making and mending clothes. All the children were taught their prayers, and Dominic paid special attention. He came to love Christ very deeply, and when he was old enough, he went to Mass every day – early, before school. Sometimes when the priest arrived for Mass, he would find Dominic kneeling outside, waiting for the church to be unlocked, even when it was bitterly cold and snowing.

Dominic worked hard at school and wanted to be a priest. He made some rules for himself, promising that he would go to confession often, that he would always make Sundays and Holy Days special, that Jesus and Mary would be his best friends, and that his motto would be "Death, rather than sin!" The teachers noticed that he never complained about things like bad weather or boring food. Dominic died when he was only fourteen. He was declared a saint in 1933, the first teenager in modern times to be canonised.

Dominic Savio was described as "small in size but a giant in spirit".

Maria Goretti

Maria Goretti lived in the first years of the twentieth century with her widowed mother and her brothers and sister on a farm which, due to their poverty, they shared with another family, the Serenellis.

One afternoon, twenty-year-old Alessandro Serenelli came to talk to Maria when she was alone. He proposed that they have sex together. Maria knew that this would be wrong, and said no. When Alessandro insisted, she refused – even when he got angry and threatened to kill her. Finally, when she said "No, No! It's a sin!" he stabbed her repeatedly. Her cries for help were finally heard and she was rushed to hospital. She had been stabbed a total of fourteen times. If she had said "Yes" she might have saved her life – but she refused to do what she knew was wrong.

Before she died, Maria forgave Alessandro. He went to prison, and while there he made a full repentance. He later joined a monastery. In 1950, Maria was canonised as a saint, and Alessandro went to the ceremony at St Peter's in Rome.

Maria Goretti is the patron saint of young people trying to live good and pure lives.

Bernadette Soubirous

Bernadette Soubirous was fourteen years old and collecting firewood near her home in the foothills of the Pyrenees in France when something extraordinary happened. There was a sudden gust of wind, and turning, she saw a beautiful young woman, standing in a cave by the river, in an area where local people dumped rubbish. The lady was holding a rosary, and asked Bernadette very courteously to return in a few days' time, which she did.

Over the next visits, the lady spoke to Bernadette, asking her to pray. She asked that a chapel be built, and for processions to be held. When Bernadette asked the lady's name, she replied "I am the Immaculate Conception", by which she meant that she was Our Lady, Christ's sinless mother. She invited Bernadette to wash from a spring nearby; there was no spring, but Bernadette scrabbled in the earth and a small trickle of water came up.

In the days that followed, a great flow of water poured out from the spot, which continues to this day: millions of people have journeyed there to pray, many sick people have been healed, and Lourdes is a place of pilgrimage, bringing together people from all over the world.

Bernadette spoke simply and truthfully about the visions at Lourdes, making no claims to be important. Through her, Our Lady was able to offer healing and hope to millions.

Don't ever think then that you are unknown to him, as if you were just a number in an anonymous crowd. Each one of you is precious to Christ, he knows you personally, he loves you tenderly, even when you are not aware of it.

Pope St John Paul II
Rome, World Youth Day 2000

Living the Christian Life

Believing • Practising • Praying

About prayer

Prayer is the easiest way to make God a part of our lives. We use prayer to thank God for our blessings, to say sorry for our sins, to ask him for his help and guidance, and to praise him with words of love. Sometimes we pray to the saints as well – especially to Mary, the Blessed Mother of Jesus – asking them to pray with us, and for us, to God.

We can pray at any time and use any words we want. Prayers can be long and fancy, using rich, old-fashioned language, or very simple, using ordinary words to talk to God. The name of Jesus can be a prayer all by itself when we can't form the words to say more. Sometimes, though, there is a traditional prayer that is just perfect for what we need to say to God. The more of these we know, the easier we find it to pray. Here are some traditional prayers that can help absolutely anyone to learn to talk to God.

Glory be to the Father, and to the Son,
and to the Holy Spirit.

We start our prayers with the Sign of the Cross:

In the name of the Father, and of the Son, and of the Holy Spirit. Amen.

Our Father

Our Father, who art in heaven, hallowed be thy name. Thy Kingdom come. Thy will be done on earth as it is in heaven. Give us this day our daily bread, and forgive us our trespasses, as we forgive those who trespass against us, and lead us not into temptation, but deliver us from evil. Amen.

Hail Mary

Hail, Mary, full of grace, the Lord is with thee. Blessed art thou among women, and blessed is the fruit of thy womb, Jesus. Holy Mary, Mother of God, pray for us sinners, now, and at the hour of our death. Amen.

Glory be

Glory be to the Father, and to the Son, and to the Holy Spirit. As it was in the beginning, is now, and ever shall be, world without end. Amen.

I Believe (The Apostles' Creed)

I believe in God,
the Father almighty,
Creator of heaven and earth,
and in Jesus Christ, his only Son, our Lord,
who was conceived by the Holy Spirit,
born of the Virgin Mary,
suffered under Pontius Pilate,
was crucified, died and was buried;
he descended into hell;
on the third day he rose again from the dead;
he ascended into heaven,
and is seated at the right hand of God
    the Father almighty;
from there he will come to judge the living and the dead.
I believe in the Holy Spirit,
the holy catholic Church,
the communion of saints,
the forgiveness of sins,
the resurrection of the body,
and life everlasting. Amen.

Prayer to the Holy Spirit

Come, O Holy Spirit, fill the hearts of your faithful, and enkindle in them the fire of your love.

V. Send forth your Spirit and they shall be created.
R. **And you shall renew the face of the earth.**

Let us pray:
O God, who taught the hearts of the faithful by the light of the Holy Spirit, grant that by the gift of the same Spirit we may be always truly wise and ever rejoice in his consolation. Through Christ our Lord.
R. **Amen.**

Prayer in the morning

We should start each day with prayer. Try saying an *Our Father*, a *Hail Mary* and a *Glory be* and then this prayer:

Lord God, may everything I do today
Begin with your inspiration
Continue with your help,
And through you come to completion.
Through Jesus Christ Our Lord. Amen.

Morning offering

O Jesus, through the most pure heart of Mary, I offer you all my prayers, thoughts, works and sufferings of this day for all the intentions of your most Sacred Heart.
O most Sacred Heart of Jesus, I place all my trust in you.
O most Sacred Heart of Jesus, I place all my trust in you.
O most Sacred Heart of Jesus, I place all my trust in you.

Prayer at night

At night, we should examine our conscience, ask God's pardon for any sins we have committed during the day, and seek his blessing as we prepare to sleep. An *Our Father*, a *Hail Mary* and a *Glory be* could then follow, and here are some prayers you could add.

May he support us all the day long
Until the shades lengthen and the evening comes
And the busy world is hushed
And the fever of life is over
And our work is done.
Then, in his mercy,
May he grant us a safe lodging
And a holy rest
And peace at the last.

St John Henry Newman

Prayer to my guardian angel

O angel of God, my guardian dear
to whom God's love commits me here.
Ever this day/night be at my side
to light, to guard, to rule and guide. Amen.

Prayer to St Michael

St Michael, the Archangel, defend us in the day of battle; be our safeguard against the wickedness and snares of the devil. May God rebuke him, we humbly pray and do you, O Prince of the heavenly host, by the power of God, cast into hell Satan and all the other evil spirits who prowl through the world seeking the ruin of souls. Amen.

Grace before meals

(three options)

✠ Bless us, O Lord, and these your gifts which we are about to receive from your bounty. Through Christ our Lord. Amen.

✠ Bless us, O God, as we sit together,
Bless the food we eat today,
Bless the hands that made the food,
Bless us, O God. Amen.

✠ Lord, we ask that you bless this food to our use
And us to your service. Amen.

Grace after meals

✠ We give you thanks, almighty God, for all your benefits, who live and reign, world without end. Amen.

✠ May the souls of the faithful departed, through the mercy of God, rest in peace. Amen.

The Memorare

Remember, O most loving Virgin Mary, that it is a thing unheard of, that anyone ever had recourse to your protection, implored your help, or sought your intercession, and was left forsaken. Filled therefore with confidence in your goodness I fly to you, O Mother, Virgin of virgins. To you I come, before you I stand, a sorrowful sinner. Despise not my poor words, O Mother of the Word of God, but graciously hear and grant my prayer.

The Hail Holy Queen

Hail, holy Queen, mother of mercy; hail, our life, our sweetness, and our hope! To you do we cry, poor banished children of Eve; to you do we send up our sighs, mourning and weeping in this vale of tears. Turn then, most gracious advocate, your eyes of mercy towards us; and after this our exile, show unto us the blessed fruit of your womb, Jesus. O clement, O loving, O sweet Virgin Mary.

V. Pray for us, O holy Mother of God.

R. **That we may be made worthy of the promises of Christ.**

Sub tuum

We fly to thy protection, O holy Mother of God. Despise not our petitions in our necessities, but deliver us always from all dangers, O glorious and blessed Virgin.

Fatima prayer

O my Jesus, forgive us our sins, save us from the fires of hell, lead all souls to heaven, especially those in most need of your mercy.

The Virgin Mother is the only woman in my life...I never fail to keep the most gracious appointment of the day – recitation of the Holy Rosary.

Blessed Carlo Acutis

Popular devotions

The Rosary

This devotion to Our Lady is probably the most popular prayer in the world. In each Mystery we meditate on an important moment in the life of Jesus while praying ten *Hail Marys*. It is good to carry rosary beads in your pocket: you can pray it anywhere, at any time.

Joyful Mysteries (Mondays and Saturdays)
1. The Annunciation
2. The Visitation
3. The Nativity
4. The Presentation of Jesus at the Temple
5. The Finding of Jesus in the Temple

Luminous Mysteries (Thursdays)
1. The Baptism in the Jordan
2. The Marriage at Cana
3. The Proclamation of the Gospel
4. The Transfiguration
5. The Institution of the Eucharist

Sorrowful Mysteries (Tuesdays and Fridays)
1. The Agony in the Garden
2. The Scourging at the Pillar
3. The Crowning with Thorns
4. The Carrying of the Cross
5. The Crucifixion and Death of Our Lord

Glorious Mysteries (Wednesdays and Sundays)
1. The Resurrection
2. The Ascension
3. The Descent of the Holy Spirit
4. The Assumption of Mary
5. The Coronation of Mary as Queen of Heaven

4th Mystery

5th Mystery

3rd Mystery

2nd Mystery
Our Father

10 Hail Marys

End

1st Mystery
Our Father

Glory Be

Glory be

3 Hail Marys

Our Father

Apostles'
Creed

Each decade of the Rosary is prayed the same way. Announce the first mystery and pray an *Our Father*. Using the beads to keep track, pray ten *Hail Marys*, then on the large bead pray a *Glory Be* and a *Fatima Prayer*. Start the next decade on the same large bead. Finish with the *Hail Holy Queen* (p. 66) and this prayer:

V. Pray for us, O holy Mother of God.

R. **That we may be made worthy of the promises of Christ.**

Let us pray:

O God, whose only-begotten Son, by his life, death and resurrection, has purchased for us the rewards of eternal life; grant, we beseech you, that meditating on these Mysteries of the most holy Rosary of the Blessed Virgin Mary, we may both imitate what they contain, and obtain what they promise, through the same Christ our Lord.

R. **Amen.**

We adore you O Christ and we bless you.

Because by your holy Cross

you have redeemed the world.

The Stations of the Cross

We 'pray the stations' during Lent. We can do this while sitting quietly at home or on a bus or train. Or we can follow the stations in church, going from each station to the next around the church.

At each station, we pray:

Leader: We adore you, O Christ, and we praise you.
All, genuflecting: **Because by your holy Cross you have redeemed the world.**

We then briefly meditate on the scene and pray:

Our Father... Hail Mary... Glory be...

Station 1   Pilate condemns Jesus to die

Station 2   Jesus accepts his Cross

Station 3   Jesus falls for the first time

Station 4   Jesus meets his mother, Mary

Station 5   Simon helps carry the Cross

Station 6   Veronica wipes the face of Jesus

Station 7   Jesus falls for the second time

Station 8   Jesus meets the women of Jerusalem

Station 9   Jesus falls for the third time

Station 10   Jesus is stripped of his clothes

Station 11   Jesus is nailed to the Cross

Station 12   Jesus dies on the Cross **(kneel for this station)**

Station 13   Jesus is taken down from the Cross

Station 14   Jesus is placed in the tomb

The Divine Mercy Chaplet

Pope St John Paul II established the feast of Divine Mercy, to be celebrated annually on the first Sunday after Easter. The *Divine Mercy Chaplet* has become popular and can be said every day on an ordinary rosary, at 3 p.m., the time of our Lord's death.

We pray it like this:

- Make the *Sign of the Cross.*
- Pray an *Our Father*, *Hail Mary* and *Apostles' Creed.*
- Then on the first big bead, say:
  "Eternal Father, I offer you the body and blood, soul and divinity of your dearly beloved Son, Our Lord, Jesus Christ, in atonement for our sins and those of the whole world."
- On each of the ten small beads, say:
  "For the sake of your sorrowful Passion, have mercy on us and on the whole world."
- Repeat for the remaining decades.
- Then say three times:
  "Holy God, Holy Mighty One, Holy Immortal One, have mercy on us and on the whole world."
- Make a final *Sign of the Cross.*

Jesus I trust in You!

Catholic doctrine

Doctrine is what we call the Truth that has been revealed by God and is then taught to subsequent generations by the Church. Doctrines are not just made up, and they are not there just for the sake of having rules. They are drawn from the Holy Scriptures, where the Word of God is recorded, and then explained to us through the careful use of human reason – in order to help us all to know God, to understand his creation and to live good lives.

To help us live as Christians every day, it is good to commit to memory, if we possibly can, some basic elements of Catholic doctrine – things like the Ten Commandments; the seven sacraments; an explanation of the Holy Trinity; and the reasons why should we go to Mass every Sunday. Knowing these things helps us to stay close to God and to know what to do and how to live well in all sorts of situations. If you ever want to know more about Catholic doctrine, or have a question about what the Church teaches about a specific topic, you can look at the *Catechism of the Catholic Church*, where it is all written down. You can find the whole Catechism at *www.vatican.va/archive/ccc/index.htm.*

The Ten Commandments

The Ten Commandments, which God revealed to Moses on Mount Sinai, tell us what is required in order to love God and our neighbour. The first three concern love of God, and the other seven love of neighbour. The Ten Commandments are a gift from God to enable us to know how to live well.

1 I am the Lord your God: you shall not have other gods before me.

2 You shall not take the name of the Lord your God in vain.

3 Remember to keep holy the Lord's Day.

4 Honour your father and your mother.

5 You shall not kill.

6 You shall not commit adultery.

7 You shall not steal.

8 You shall not bear false witness against your neighbour.

9 You shall not covet your neighbour's wife.

10 You shall not covet your neighbour's goods.

The seven sacraments touch all the stages and all the important moments of Christian life: they give birth and increase, healing and mission to the Christian's life of faith.

Catechism of the Catholic Church 1210

The Seven Sacraments

Sacraments are ceremonies that are visible signs of God's love and support for us – in other words his 'grace'. The sacraments were given to us by Jesus Christ and are administered by the Church. Each sacrament has its own deep, clear symbolism and the real effect of giving us a particular form of God's saving grace, unique to that sacrament. For example, the use of water in the sacrament of Baptism symbolises life and washing; and in Baptism we truly are given life in Christ and cleansed of the sin that separates us from him. There are seven sacraments:

1 Baptism
2 Confirmation
3 Holy Eucharist
4 Penance
5 Anointing of the Sick
6 Holy Orders
7 Matrimony

The Five Precepts of the Church

There are five duties a Catholic is required to undertake:

1 To attend Mass on Sundays and
  Holy Days of Obligation.
2 To go to Confession at least once a year.
3 To receive Holy Communion during
  the Easter season.
4 To observe the days of fasting and abstinence
  established by the Church.
5 To help to provide for the needs of the Church.

The Sacrament of Penance

This sacrament is known by several different names: Confession, Reconciliation, or simply Penance. YOUCAT, which is a book for young people that explains Catholic doctrine, has a wonderful explanation of why we Catholics confess our sins regularly:

> Jesus himself instituted the sacrament of Penance when he showed himself to his Apostles on Easter day and commanded them: "Receive the Holy Spirit. If you forgive the sins of any they are forgiven; if you retain the sins of any they are retained." Nowhere did Jesus express more beautifully what happens in the sacrament of Penance than in the parable of the Prodigal Son: we go astray, we are lost and can no longer cope. Yet our Father waits for us with great, indeed, infinite longing; he forgives us when we come back, he takes us in again, forgives our sins. Jesus himself forgave the sins of many individuals; it was more important to him than working miracles. He regarded this as the great sign of the dawning of the Kingdom of God, in which all wounds are healed and all tears wiped away. Jesus forgave sins in the power of the Holy Spirit, and he handed this power on to his Apostles. We fall into the arms of our heavenly Father when we go to a priest and confess (*YOUCAT* 227).

Going to Confession:

Find out when confessions are being heard in a church near you.

• Kneel down and think about sins you have committed and ask for God's forgiveness and pardon. Sometimes it is helpful to do what is called an 'examination of conscience', which is a series of questions you ask yourself to help you recall your sins so that you can make a good confession. There is an examination of conscience designed for young people like you on p. 80.

• When your turn comes, kneel and say:

"Father, bless me, for I have sinned. My last confession was...[then say approximately how long ago it was: e.g., two months ago, a year ago]"

• Tell your sins briefly and simply, and when the priest asks you to, make an act of contrition.

An act of contrition

O my God, because you are so good, I am very sorry that I have sinned against you, and by the help of your grace I will not sin again.

• Listen to the words of absolution (when the priest tells you that your sins are forgiven), making the *Sign of the Cross* at the words "In the name of the Father...", and listen to any advice the priest may give you. Then say "Thank you" and leave.

• Kneel and pray your penance, then pray for the priest who gave you absolution.

An Examination of Conscience

Always begin an examination of conscience in prayer, asking God to help you to know your sins. Then it might help to ask yourself a series of questions like this:

- Did I purposefully think of other things during prayer, or cut prayer out so that I could do other things?

- Did I miss or arrive late for Sunday (or Saturday vigil) Mass through my own fault?

- Did I disobey my parents or teachers? Did I answer back or treat them disrespectfully?

- Did I treat anyone unkindly? Did I encourage or go along with others when they were unkind?

- Was I angry or resentful? Did I fight or quarrel? Did I keep mean or angry thoughts in my mind on purpose?

- Did I call other people names or say bad words? Did I use the name of God or Jesus without respect?

- Did I purposefully look at bad pictures or videos online, or watch TV programmes, read books or play computer games with bad content?

- Did I do anything shameful, or anything that is only allowed in marriage, by myself or with anyone else? Did I keep impure thoughts in my mind on purpose?

- Did I steal or tell someone else to steal? Did I keep something that wasn't mine?

- Did I damage or destroy anything belonging to someone else on purpose?

- Did I tell lies? Did I conceal anything bad from my parents or teachers?

The Mass

Sunday Mass is the most important action of the week. If we are travelling, or visiting friends, it is easy to find out the Mass times at a convenient Catholic church: we can check it out on the internet beforehand.

We should never miss Sunday Mass unless we are not well or some major event prevents us from getting to the church.

But why is Sunday Mass so important? Just think of what Jesus has done for us, and how in a special way he is present 24/7 in our churches. Can we really not be bothered to be with him once a week on the day that he rose from the dead? Surely we can!

Making a Spiritual Communion

Sometimes you may not be able to receive Holy Communion. You may not have fasted as much as an hour, or you may be far from a church, or there may be some other reason. In such a case, it is good to make a spiritual Communion, which is when we pray to join our hearts with Jesus's through the sacrifice of the Eucharist.

St Alphonsus Liguori's Spiritual Communion Prayer

My Jesus, I believe that you are present in the most Blessed Sacrament. I love you above all things and I desire to receive you into my soul. Since I cannot now receive you sacramentally, come at least spiritually into my heart. I embrace you as if you were already there, and unite myself wholly to you. Never permit me to be separated from you. Amen.

Adore with Seraph's love,
my Jesus hidden in the host
come down from heaven above.
O bring my Lord to me,
that his sweet Heart may rest on mine,
and I his temple be.

Adoration of the Blessed Sacrament

Jesus is present in the Blessed Sacrament in the tabernacle in every Catholic church. We can visit him there whenever the church is open. We should make use of every opportunity.

If the Blessed Sacrament is brought out for adoration, we should make a special effort to pay a visit. We could encourage friends to come, too.

Pray using some of the prayers from this book – or just speak to Christ silently in your own words.

In his 2010 Westminster Cathedral *Message to Young People*, Pope Benedict spoke of the need for moments of silence and prayer in our busy lives:

> Every day we have to choose to love – and this requires help, the help that comes from Christ, from prayer and from the wisdom found in his word, and from the grace which he bestows on us in the sacraments of his Church.
>
> This is the message I want to share with you today. I ask you to look into your hearts, each day, to find the source of all true love. Jesus is always there, quietly waiting for us to be still with him and to hear his voice. Deep within your heart, he is calling you to spend time with him in prayer. But this kind of prayer, real prayer, requires discipline; it requires making time for moments of silence every day. Often it means waiting for the Lord to speak. Even amidst the 'busy-ness' and the stress of our daily lives, we need to make space for silence, because it is in silence that we find God, and in silence that we discover our true self.

Creator of all things,
true source of light and wisdom,
give me a sharp sense of understanding,
a retentive memory, and the ability to
grasp things correctly and fundamentally.
Grant me the talent of being exact in
my explanations, and the ability to express
myself with thoroughness and charm.
Point out the beginning, direct the
progress, and help in completion;
through Christ our Lord. Amen.

From St Thomas Aquinas's
Prayer Before Study

Quick
Queries

Why are there different Christian denominations? Can't all Christians just unite?

Of course we should all get together. In his Encyclical Letter on ecumenism (the unity of Christians), *Ut Unum Sint*, Pope St John Paul II stresses that through baptism all Christians "belong to Christ" (n. 42), and reminds us of our duty as Christians to love each other. But there are genuine differences about some important things. We can't just force people to join the Catholic Church if they genuinely disagree with what the Church teaches; but likewise, we cannot just join another Christian denomination, thinking they are all more or less the same. There are some important differences.

For example, some Christians believe that when you die, you will simply go straight to heaven or hell: there is no opportunity to be cleansed of your sins and people cannot pray for you. Some even believe that God has planned in advance who will be chosen for heaven: so you cannot go there if you are not among that number.

The Catholic Church understands that we will each be judged when we meet God, and that we can be helped by the loving prayers of people still alive. Purgatory is a place of cleansing. God is merciful.

In addition to differences in doctrine, there are some very important differences in practice amongst Christians. In the Catholic Church, the sacraments are at the very heart of how we practise our faith, particularly the Eucharist, which we celebrate at every Mass as Jesus commanded, and which we know to be his true body, blood, soul and divinity, because he revealed this great truth to us. By contrast, many other Christians believe that the Eucharist is just a symbol, which makes how they pray and worship different. St John Henry Newman, when he was still an Anglican, was stunned to discover that the Eucharist was kept in the tabernacle of every Catholic church, making Catholic churches *true* temples, places where God truly dwells.

However, despite our differences, all Christians should try to listen to one another and treat one another with respect. Catholics honour some great men and women of other Christian denominations, such as the great preachers and hymn-writers John and Charles Wesley, and the anti-slavery campaigner William Wilberforce, all of whom were strong Evangelical Christians.

We should pray for Christian unity together with other Christians. John Paul II wrote in *Ut Unum Sint* that Christian love "finds its most complete expression in common prayer." (n. 21) Prayer is so powerful that he claimed: "If Christians, despite their divisions can grow ever more united in common prayer around Christ, they will grow in awareness of how little divides them in comparison to what unites them." (n. 22)

Why must we go to Mass on Sundays?

The Church's law is that all Catholics must attend Mass on Sundays and Holy Days of Obligation. Of course, there are some Sundays when we can't make it because of illness or an emergency. On most Sundays, however, most of us can and should attend Mass. Many parishes also have a Vigil Mass on Saturday evening that counts for Sunday, so it is possible for most of us to get to Mass every week, even if our Sundays are busy.

In St Paul's first letter to the Corinthians, we read that Jesus "...on the night when he was betrayed, took bread, and when he had given thanks, ...broke it, and said, 'This is my body which is for you. Do this in remembrance of me.'" Mass is where the sacrifice of the Eucharist happens, and so in asking us to do this in order to remember him, Jesus invites us to Mass.

In every Mass we encounter Jesus in the Word of God proclaimed through the Bible readings, and again when he becomes present on the altar in the consecrated bread and wine.

Why do Holy Days matter?

In our families and communities we celebrate special days together. Days like birthdays, or the anniversaries of marriages or special events in society (coronations, victories in important battles, the end of a war) are a cause for celebration. We also make time to mark sad events like deaths. The Church is also a family with important things to celebrate and commemorate. The Church's calendar follows the birth, death, and Resurrection of Christ, his Ascension into heaven, and the coming of the Holy Spirit at Pentecost.

As Catholics, we must do our best to attend and take part in Holy Mass every Sunday. That, together with attendance at Mass on certain other important days, is required of us as a minimum. So, in addition to Sundays, the Church marks various days – including Epiphany and the Ascension – as especially holy and adds the feasts of various saints. In addition to the major feasts, different countries have their own special feast days. In England, Wales and Scotland these are:

- Epiphany (6th January)
- Ascension
- Saints Peter and Paul (29th June)
- Assumption of Our Lady (15th August)
- All Saints (1st November)
- Christmas Day (25th December)
- In Ireland, St Patrick's Day (17th March) is added.

We should attend Mass on these days – and have a real celebration too! The Church is alive: we are not just marking things that happened long ago.

How does the Church's calendar work?

The Church's calendar, which tracks the 'liturgical year' is made up of different seasons that give us a particular focus for our prayer and worship. The Church year begins with Advent, during which we prepare to celebrate the birth of Christ. This is followed by the Christmas season, which is not just Christmas Day, but lasts into January. Then there is a period of what we call 'Ordinary Time' before Lent – a penitential season culminating in Holy Week – begins, followed by the Easter Season, then Pentecost, and then a long stretch of Ordinary Time through to the next Advent.

At Mass you will *see* the seasons marked by the priest's different coloured vestments: purple and pink for Advent and Lent, white for Christmas, Easter and many great feasts, red for Good Friday and Pentecost, and green for Ordinary Time. You will also *hear* the changing focus of the seasons in the prayers and readings of the Mass: each year the Church follows cycles of penance and grief and of celebration and rejoicing.

Finding out how the calendar works is fascinating. The big seasons of Christmas and Easter up to the feast of the Ascension are forty days long, and so is Lent. The number forty seems to be written into us: it's the number of weeks a child lives in the womb; the Israelites spent forty years in the desert seeking the Promised Land; and Christ spent forty days in prayer in the desert before starting his public ministry.

Ascension Day is celebrated forty days after Easter Sunday and is always on a Thursday in England, Wales and Scotland. In many countries it is honoured as a public holiday.

There are then nine days between Ascension Day and Pentecost: the Bible tells us that the Apostles spent the days following the Ascension in prayer, and then the Holy Spirit came to them at Pentecost. That's the origin of our tradition of having a *novena*, nine days of prayer, when we need to pray about something special.

'Pente' means fifty: Pentecost is fifty days after Easter and is another festival of celebration as it marks the descent of the Holy Spirit on the disciples and thus the beginning of the Church's mission to preach Jesus's message to the world.

Are priests always holy?

No. Priests are normal men: being ordained doesn't mean that you will never sin! There are thousands of Catholic priests around the world, doing good and holy work. But of course they are human beings like everyone else, and are capable of committing sins.

Priests are called to a high standard: we quite rightly expect them to be holy and to be completely dedicated to God and to the work they have been called to do. We should pray for our priests: like everyone else, they can be tempted to do evil.

A priest who commits serious sins, including sexual sins, can be formally 'laicised' – that is, made to leave the priesthood.

Why are all priests men?

Jesus chose only men to be his Apostles – in contrast to all the pagan religions of his time and place, which had priestesses (or women priests). Just as he broke normal rules when he walked on water, multiplied loaves and fishes, and used his spittle to heal the blind, so he did something specific in calling only men to be his ministers. The priesthood is about service: men serving God's people in the Church. The Apostles were not chosen because they were holier than anyone else – we learn about them quarrelling among themselves, and such like.

God's whole plan from the beginning is likened in the Bible to a marriage relationship, which is between a male and a female. The Church is his 'Bride', and from this union of Christ and Church there are now millions of children. That's why we speak of 'Holy Mother Church'.

And creating us as male and female has a much deeper meaning than we might at first think. Above all, a woman gave birth to God in human form: Jesus's genes came from Mary, and she is unique in the human race, something no man could achieve. Mary is an image of the Church.

Are men and women different?

Being male or female is not just a matter of feelings. We are different in every part of our bodies, in the very chromosomes of which we are made. It is the coming together of a man and a woman that brings new life. God planned this from the beginning, and this central truth about the significance of male and female rings through our salvation story: man and woman, Bridegroom and Bride, Christ and his Church.

What does the Church teach about LGBT people?

The Church teaches that some actions and activities are forbidden, even if we really want to do them. YOUCAT has this to say about the Church's teachings on homosexuality:

> God created [humanity] as male and female and destined them for each other in a bodily way as well. The Church accepts without reservation those who experience homosexual feelings. They (persons who experience homosexual feelings) should not be unjustly discriminated against because of that. At the same time, the Church declares that all homosexual relations in any form are contrary to the order of creation (*YOUCAT* 415).

Why is there suffering in the world?

In the beginning, when God brought everything into being, it was perfect. He created men and women to be perfectly happy and gave them everything, inviting them to share fully in his love. But above all he made them free: they were not machines that were just switched on to a set path. They could choose whether or not to love him. They chose not to, and so sin came into the world: the perfection was broken and suffering entered into human life and into the natural world.

We call this 'Original Sin', and the Bible (Genesis) describes it, using figurative language. The Bible also describes how God then acted. The original plan was damaged, but in order to mend our relationship with him, God chose to come and live among us, now accepting suffering along with us.

Suffering is part of being human: when God chose to live among us as a human being, he suffered, including a long-drawn-out tortuous death on the Cross. God is wholly good and perfect; by accepting suffering he accepted the fullness of human existence and taught us at the very deepest level what it means to be human. He also taught us, through his miracles of healing, that suffering is not his original plan, that we can work to alleviate suffering, and that we can also hope for an eternity with him where there is no pain and all is peace and joy.

Have Catholics always behaved well?

No. Here on earth we are a Church of sinners as well as saints. Christ guaranteed that the Church would always teach the truth. But he knew that the people involved would not always be holy. There have been popes, bishops and priests who behaved badly. There is a difference between Holy Mother Church and her sinful children.

On the First Sunday of Lent in the year 2000, Pope St John Paul II led a service of repentance at St Peter's in Rome, expressing sorrow for sins and mistakes committed in the name of the Church over previous centuries. It included a statement that "even men of the Church, in the name of faith and morals, have sometimes used methods not in keeping with the Gospel in the solemn duty of defending the truth" and acknowledged that "in certain periods of history, Christians have at times given in to intolerance and have not been faithful to the great commandment of love, sullying in this way the face of the Church".

Are the internet and modern technology good?

Much of life happens online these days, and the majority of communication for many young people takes place using mobile phones. Our mobile phones mean that we can watch things from all over the world, and send and receive anything from our friends, or even from strangers.

Being able to form friendships with a huge variety of people can be a wonderful thing, and the ease of communications can strengthen existing communities. But, on the other hand, not all people are good or have good intentions. Predatory people can use the internet to meet children and young people to abuse or exploit; and even if we don't talk to strangers at all, many people have heart-breaking experience of online bullying.

All the advances in technology mean that we have access to a huge amount of information instantly, anywhere we go: we can 'Google' anything we want to know. This can be dangerous as well as being helpful: there is a lot of false and harmful information masquerading as the truth online, and if you don't know anything about the topic, you won't be able to determine whether what you are reading is true. Even images can be edited, giving us a completely false idea of beauty and causing terrible insecurity and mental health problems for many people. Also, looking at strong sexual images or terrible violence can affect people's minds, hearts and relationships badly.

It's important to use digital devices wisely: they are tools, and you should be in control. Be strong minded: if you come across nude pictures, crude language or vicious talk, click off at once. If you feel as if you aren't in control, are addicted to bad online content, or are becoming angry, sad, fearful or anxious because of things you see online, ask for help!

Are saints always people from long ago?

No. God raises up saints in every century. There are people alive today who worked with Pope St John Paul II in Poland and in Rome, or with Fr Jerzy Popieluscko, or with St Mother Teresa in the various places where she established homes for the poor and sick.

There were saints who lived during World War II, including St Edith Stein, who perished in Auschwitz. There were saints in the time of Queen Victoria, such as St John Henry Newman, who lived when Britain was a major industrial country with steamships and railways and factories.

There are young people growing up today who will one day perhaps be declared saints and add their own part to the ongoing story of the Church.

One day Christ will return, and we will discover about all the saints who served him – including many who were completely unknown.

Top: St Edith Stein, Bl. Jerzy Popieluscko, St John Paul II
Bottom: Bl. Cyprian Tansi, St Gianna Beretta Molla and Bl. Pier Giorgio Frassati

*We have come to believe in God's love:
in these words the Christian can express
the fundamental decision of his life.
Being Christian is not the result of
an ethical choice or a lofty idea, but the
encounter with an EVENT, A PERSON,
which gives life a new horizon and
a decisive direction.*

Pope Benedict XVI
Deus Caritas Est

Over to YOU

What could help you to be a better Catholic?

First things first

- Get a copy of the *Catechism of the Catholic Church* or find it online at *www.vatican.va/archive/ccc/index.htm* and challenge yourself to look up topics on which you have questions.

- Go to a weekday Mass on your own or with a friend.

- Read a chapter of the Bible daily.

- Read about the lives of the saints.

- Keep a journal of prayers/letters from you to God.

- Ask your RE teacher if you can invite a Catholic speaker into your school, or a team of missionaries from NET Ministries.

- Volunteer to help others.

- Say morning and evening prayers.

- Pray the Rosary every day.

- Offer up all your actions to God every morning.

- Use your creativity to do Christian arts and crafts, for example:

  - Rosary beads
  - Paintings
  - Drawings
  - Jewellery
  - Prayer garden
  - Prayer cards
  - Mosaics
  - Cross stitch
  - Painting candle holders
  - Creating your own handmade prayer book.

Watch and listen: TV, video, radio, film and theatre

As you can imagine, in today's world of media overload, it can be difficult to find the right resources, amidst the sea of entertainment, information and educational resources out there, to help you explore and live out your faith. You could dip your toe in the water by:

- Finding out about what you can watch on EWTN (Eternal Word Television Network).

- Finding out what you can listen to on the latest version of *Radio Maria* that has been set up in Britain.

- Checking out *The Chosen* – a new multi-season series about the life of Christ. Two seasons have aired already, and a further five are in various stages of development. The series is available on YouTube all over the world, and the free app can be downloaded to your phone or digital TV.

- Looking out for more things to watch and listen to. Below you will find some suggestions.

Films for young people

A Man for All Seasons (1966) U

The Nun's Story (1959) PG

Bahkita: From Slave to Saint (2009) Unrated

Blue Miracle (2021) PG

Don Bosco (1988) Unrated

Fatima (2020) 12

Heaven is for Real (2014) PG

It's a Wonderful Life (1946) U

Jesus of Nazareth (1977) Unrated

Joseph: King of Dreams (2000) U

Karol – A Man Who Became Pope (2005) Unrated

Lilies of the Field (1963) U

Miracle of Marcelino (1955) U

Molokai: The Story of Father Damien (1999) PG

Mother Teresa (2003) Unrated

Of Gods and Men (2010) 15

Pius XII: Under the Roman Sky (2010) Unrated

Prince of Egypt (1998) U

St Giuseppe Moscati: Doctor to the Poor (2009) Unrated

The Ten Commandments (1956) U

There Be Dragons (2011) 15

The Reluctant Saint (1962) U

The Robe (1953) U

The Scarlet and the Black (1983) PG

The Star (2017) U

Radio stations/podcasts for young people

The social media landscape is constantly evolving, but at the time of printing, these are some of the best Catholic podcasts and media outlets available.

EWTN Youth:
https://www.ewtn.com/catholicism/library/youth-866

Pints with Aquinas podcast:
Ever wanted to sit down with St Thomas Aquinas (a saint who was pretty smart at all things theology: check out his *Summa Theologica* if you're feeling daring)? In this podcast, Matt Fradd sits down and discusses topics from the *Summa Theologica* he'd address if he had a chance to talk with St Thomas Aquinas himself.

The Fr Mike Schmitz Catholic Podcast:
Fr Mike Schmitz talks about faith, pop culture and headlines on this podcast. If you've got 8–10 minutes sometime, this is a great podcast to dive into.

The Word on Fire Show podcast:
Bishop Robert Barron sits down to discuss things happening in the Church and topics related to the Catholic Faith.

Integrity Restored podcast:
This podcast will equip you with the knowledge and resources you need to live a porn-free life and to help others do the same.

The Bible in a Year podcast:
The readings and reflections for each day will help deepen your love of the Scriptures and appreciate those hard-to-read books like Leviticus. If you are leading any kind of Bible study, this is a must-listen.

The Catholic Talk Show podcast:
An informative and hilarious Catholic podcast.

The Crunch Catholic Podcast:
Pat and Ethan sit down and talk about the Catholic faith in this podcast. They share their life and witness to the Gospel and, as well as talking with young Catholics, they have some very interesting and influential guests join them on their show.

How-to Catholic podcast:
Do you love how-to videos on YouTube? If you do, you'll love this podcast from Lisa and Kevin Cotter. They conquer every question about how to live the Catholic life, as well as why and how to do anything in life from a Catholic perspective.

Do Something Beautiful podcast:
Leah Darrow, former model and contestant on America's Next Top Model, shares stories of people in the world who are doing something beautiful for Christ and encourages listeners to do something beautiful for Christ with their own lives.

Catholic Stuff You Should Know podcast:
An ongoing discussion of relevant and interesting Catholic topics.

The Catholic Current podcast:
Bringing Christ to the world and the world to Christ.

Catholic Youth Ministry Podcast:
A technology, Christianity, spirituality, religion and education podcast from two youth ministers, Edmund Mitchell and Nic Guiterrez.

The Wintershall plays

Look up this theatre group. You might be able to go to see one of their amazing performances. GO FOR IT!

The *Life of Christ* is a powerful biblical outdoor drama staged at a whole-day event in Surrey, with some people camping overnight.

Each year on Good Friday, the *Passion of Jesus*, a play about Jesus's last hours in our world, is performed in Trafalgar Square, in London, with two performances. These are both productions performed by the Wintershall theatre group.

Get involved!

One of the best things about being a Catholic is how it brings people together. The Catholic Church is a community of people united in Christ. It is more than just a building! It can be a bit daunting to take the first steps to becoming involved, but remember that Jesus walks with you and will guide you.

Get together with friends

- Make a video of your own on a Christian topic. Write a script, rehearse, and produce it. Decide when and how to launch it.
- Experience faith in action – pray with friends or plan something to bring goodwill locally, such as songs and music at a local care home, a clean-up of litter in a park, or house-to-house carol-singing at Christmas.

Your local church...and further afield

Do you know what goes on at your church that young people can take part in? If you don't, then FIND OUT!

Nothing going on that interests you? Then start something! Ask others, ask Father. DO IT!

Some parishes have a junior St Vincent de Paul Society (Mini Vinnies), often accompanying a more senior one. You might be able to visit lonely elderly people or people in hospital, and perhaps help to give out food to homeless people. Some parishes have a young persons' Legion of Mary, which does worthwhile work and would bring you good friends.

If the church you usually attend has nothing like this, and you are interested, you could ask Father, and perhaps you could start something useful, with just one or two others. Or you could look further afield and contact a nationwide Catholic youth network such as:

- *Youth 2000*, which is very active with different events and pilgrimages.
- *The Faith Movement*, which hosts talks in London and Glasgow throughout the year and runs summer breaks for young people aged 11 to 15 and youth days for the 11 to 18 age group, as well as a winter break over the Christmas holiday period.

Find out about going on a pilgrimage

In England there is the national shrine at Walsingham in Norfolk where many young people go, often for a full weekend. In Scotland large groups gather at the shrine of Carfin near Glasgow. In Wales the shrine at Holywell is extremely popular. In Ireland, the shrine at Knock even has its own airport.

Looking further: teams of young people from every diocese in Britain travel regularly with the sick and disabled to Lourdes as helpers combining practical help with friendship and shared prayer and rich experiences. The shrine at Lourdes began when young St Bernadette obeyed the request from Our Lady to scrabble in the earth – a healing spring bubbled up which has never stopped. At Fatima in Portugal Our Lady appeared to three young people in 1917 with a powerful message and since then millions have gathered there year on year. Groups of pilgrims also travel from Britain to Chartres in France each Pentecost, to the famous shrine at Compostella in Spain and to Czestochowa in Poland.

Go deeper!

Great reads: visit www.ctsbooks.org

- *The Catechism of the Catholic Church*
- *Gospel of St Luke*
- *A Simple Prayer Book*
- *Youcat*
- *Sycamore: The Catholic Faith Explained*
- *Online with Saints*

Catholic websites for young people

https://lifeteen.com
https://www.youcat.org
https://www.catholicvoices.org.uk
https://www.youth2000.org
https://www.faith.org.uk
https://www.onlinewithsaints.com
https://www.catholic.com
https://www.churchpop.com

YouTube pages for young Catholics

Pints with Aquinas:
https://www.youtube.com/c/PintsWithAquinas

Ascension Presents:
https://www.youtube.com/c/AscensionPresents

The Bible in a Year:
*https://www.youtube.com/
channelUCzUZD3iCxkHmwYkCq Yn8fBw*

Sensus Fidelium:
https://www.youtube.com/c/SensusFidelium

Dynamic Catholic:
https://www.youtube.com/user/DynamicCatholic

Word on Fire Institute:
https://www.youtube.com/c/WordonFireInstitute

Youth 2000:
https://www.youtube.com/c/Youth2000uk

Life Teen:
https://www.youtube.com/user/LifeTeenInc

Catholic Answers:
https://www.youtube.com/user/catholiccom

FOCUS Catholic:
https://www.youtube.com/c/FOCUSCatholic

Shalom TV:
https://www.youtube.com/watch?v=jvbRAliRmQg

Catholic social media pages to follow

@catholicconnect
@catholicfaithformation
@catholic_teen_posts
@catholicmemes
@litcatholicmemes
@catholicanswers
@ctspublishers
@wordonfire_catholicministries
@catholicammo
@ewtnmedia
@fathermikeschmitz
@catholictalkshow
@youth2000uk
@focuscatholic
@netministries

Trust in God

Whatever happens, all our lives long, we can trust God and turn to him in good times and in bad. He loves us, more than we can possibly imagine, and he wants what is good and beautiful for us.

DO NOT BE AFRAID

These words are a direct call to us. St John Paul II – the Pope who led the Church across the threshold of the twenty first century – made this call his message to the world, and especially to the young. We can trust God to guide, guard and protect us, no matter what happens.

It is good to follow Jesus; it's good to discover the great love He has for each one of us; it's good to venture into the project of happiness He has planned for me, for you, for everyone; it's good to discover the gifts He gives us with great generosity, the surprises that fill our lives with wonder and hope, that make us grow free and happy.

Pope Francis

PICTURE CREDITS: